Foreword by Chris Baines

The world is full of wonderful wildlife, but you might think all the really exciting creatures live in other far away countries. Wildlife in Great Britain is perhaps not quite so spectacular as that of Africa or the Arctic, but as you'll discover when you use this book, our wildlife is still pretty amazing – and you can enjoy it without being eaten alive or freezing to death! The wildlife that is living right on our doorstep is very special, and with a bit of help, you can find something new each time you take a look.

Many wild animals hide away during the day and only creep out after dark. That makes them difficult to watch, but if you know where to look, you can find plenty of evidence that foxes and hedgehogs, badgers and woodmice are in the area. If you hunt around where you live, you'll find you're sharing it with all kinds of other creatures. Put out food for some of them, and you might be lucky enough to see them. It's especially good to creep out on a warm summer's night, as late as you can, and sit very quietly, listening to all the rustlings in the undergrowth. Take a torch and shine it into the depths of your local pond. You'll see all kinds of animals there that stay hidden in the daytime.

You need a mixture of habitats to study if you are going to find lots of different wildlife – and the best places are the wild corners where few people go. Overgrown churchyards, abandoned quarries, weedy, tangled gardens, woodlands thick with undergrowth: these are the places to look for wildlife.

Go to the right kind of habitat, sit very still and silent, and wait for the wildlife to come to you. If you can blend into the background, quite shy creatures will accept you as part of the landscape. I've had badgers walk over my feet before now and a fox club wander to within a metre before its nose sniffed me on the breeze.

We talk about *watching* wildlife – but listening is just as important. Birds are easy to see, because they're active in the daytime, but even so, a good wildlife watcher will usually *hear* a particular bird before spotting it. Kingfishers have a piercing whistle, kestrels mew like cats, and tiny wrens make an enormous racket as they creep about, camouflaged amongst the undergrowth and singing to defend their territory.

Birds can't hibernate. Many of our birds are out and about all year round – indeed the cold winter weather makes them hungry and they become even less timid as they search for food. Some birds do something much more exciting: they migrate. Lots of our common summer birds fly 4,000 miles south, to spend the winter on the wing in sunny Africa, and, as soon as they leave us at the end of summer, millions of other birds arrive here from colder countries to the north. If you see starlings fighting over crumbs outside your window, most of them will probably be here for the winter, but will fly off to northern Russia in the spring. That's where they build their nests and lay their eggs – although a few million starlings do stay here all year round.

I think it's very exciting to know that by making my patch a pesticide-free zone in the summer, I can ensure there are plenty of caterpillars for the birds to eat, and by putting out nuts and fat and fruit in the winter, I am helping wildlife on an international scale. We may not have the world's most spectacular wildlife here, but our swallows spend the winter snapping up the flies around the lions, hippos and giraffes of Africa. Our redwings, fieldfares and other winter birds may well see polar bears and reindeer as they fly north to build their nests in Greenland or northern Russia.

We have rare and endangered species in Great Britain too. Some of our bats are almost extinct, we have very rare lizards, toads and newts, and many of our wild creatures are suffering from loss of habitat here, as much as anywhere in the world.

This book should help you get close to wildlife. Once you begin to understand how important the different habitats are, you can help to make the place where you live a better, safer area for wildlife. If you can do that, then it will be a much better place for us to live too – and you'll have done your bit to help with wildlife conservation.

January

Whatever the weather is like in January, an increasing number of wild birds come nearer to our homes looking for food. Robins and members of the tit family become particularly bold. You might also see more of shy woodland species such as woodpeckers and nuthatches around bird-tables, as well as visitors from further north, such as fieldfares, redwings and starlings. During a hard winter many birds die. Food is much more difficult to find if everything is covered with ice and snow. Water birds such as kingfishers and herons suffer badly when ponds, lakes and streams are frozen over.

Insect-eating mammals, like the hedgehog and bat, spend the winter asleep, hibernating in a sheltered place. The hedgehog may wake up, though, if the weather turns mild. The dormouse makes a nest in a tree or hole in the ground. When hibernating, its body temperature

 blackbird  lesser spotted woodpecker great tit starling

mole

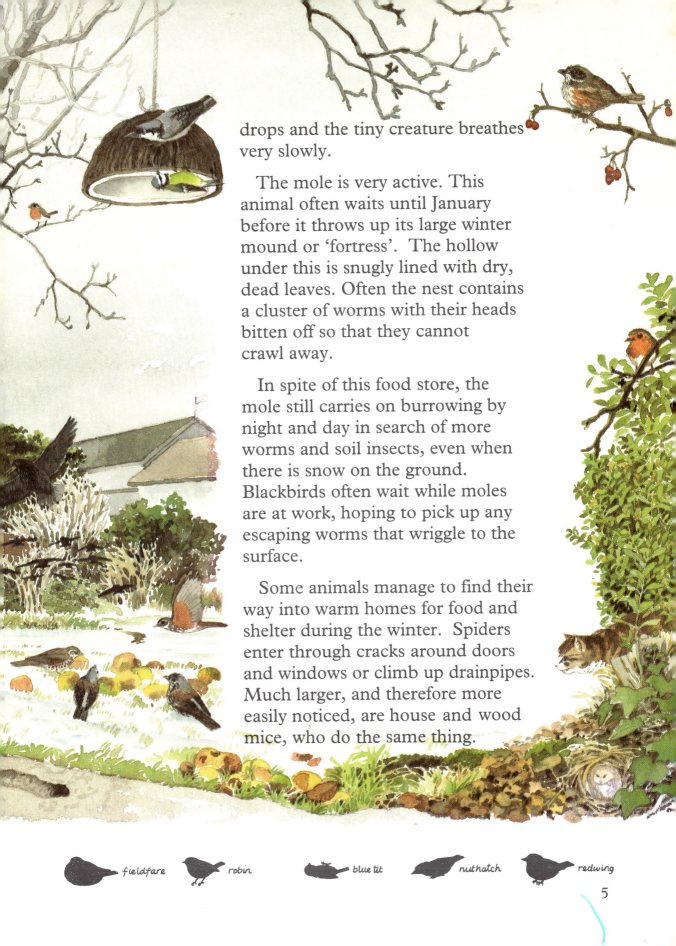

drops and the tiny creature breathes very slowly.

The mole is very active. This animal often waits until January before it throws up its large winter mound or 'fortress'. The hollow under this is snugly lined with dry, dead leaves. Often the nest contains a cluster of worms with their heads bitten off so that they cannot crawl away.

In spite of this food store, the mole still carries on burrowing by night and day in search of more worms and soil insects, even when there is snow on the ground. Blackbirds often wait while moles are at work, hoping to pick up any escaping worms that wriggle to the surface.

Some animals manage to find their way into warm homes for food and shelter during the winter. Spiders enter through cracks around doors and windows or climb up drainpipes. Much larger, and therefore more easily noticed, are house and wood mice, who do the same thing.

fieldfare   robin   blue tit   nuthatch   redwing

5

Building a bird-table

Along with an adult's help, you will need: a wooden board 50cm x 30cm, wooden strips, a wooden stake (about 1.5m long), nails, waterproof paint or varnish, scraps of food.

Nail the wooden strips around the board, but leave gaps at the corners. The table can then easily be swept clean and the rain-water will be able to run away. Paint the top of your bird-table with waterproof paint or varnish before you use it.

With an adult, carefully nail the table-top to the end of your wooden stake. Dig a hole and firmly fix the stake in the ground. Choose a spot where you can see the table easily, but don't put it too near bushes and trees where cats and grey squirrels can hide.

Each day put breadcrumbs, cake crumbs, bacon rind, cooked potato and other scraps on your bird-table. Do not feed the birds salted nuts or dried coconut: these could kill them. Only feed the birds during the winter months when food is scarce.

Making bird feeders

Along with an adult's help, you will need: a sharp knife, an old, plastic lemonade bottle, string, an old piece of wood, nails, metal bottle tops, a screw-eye, scraps of food and fat.

Ask an adult to cut two round holes in your bottle. Make a hole in the top of it so that you can hang it up. Put food in the bottom of the bottle.

Take a short piece of wood. Nail the bottle tops along it. Put a screw-eye in one end. Fill the bottle tops with fat and hang up your feeder.

Which birds visit your feeders?

6

Watch how they take the food.
Do they peck off little bits of food
or do they take large lumps and fly
off with them?

Which foods do birds like best?

You will need: a small plank of wood,
five or six lids, different scraps
of food.

Place your lids on the wood and set it
down on the ground where you can see

it clearly, but away from trees and
bushes.

Put a different food in each lid: try
breadcrumbs, fat, bacon rind, seeds,
cheese or cooked potato, for example.

Watch carefully and see which kind
of bird eats what food. You could make a
record of your findings and also
experiment with different foods.

7

Drinking water for birds

You will need: a shallow container.

No matter how cold the weather is, birds still like to bathe and drink. Any shallow container will do, but a dustbin lid buried in the soil works perfectly.

Keep a record in your notebook of which birds come to your pool to bathe and drink; include the time of day and the weather conditions.

Bird puddings

Along with an adult's help, you will need: a basin, a spoon, a mix of seeds, sultanas and currants, nuts, large crumbs, scraps of cheese, melted fat or suet, a coconut shell or a small flowerpot, string.

Half fill a small basin with a mixture of the above ingredients. Stir in the same amount of melted fat or suet. You can either leave the mixture to set solid in the basin, then turn it out on to the bird-table, or, while the mixture is still sticky, spoon it tightly into a coconut shell or small flowerpot and hang it up outside.

A mole weighing about 100g can excavate 5kg of soil in 20 minutes.

January

February

On bright days in February, honey bees and queen bumble bees may be gathering pollen and nectar from early flowers.

There are not many other insects about. The minotaur beetle, a large black insect that feeds on dung, can often be seen near rabbit droppings. On warm, sunny days small clusters of ladybirds may awake from hibernation and sun themselves on

 black-headed gull

 wood pigeon

 ladybird

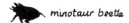 minotaur beetle

tree stumps or fence posts. At dusk, particularly after a sunny day, swarms of winter gnats dance up and down.

You might hear the male robin's plaintive song warning other robins that he is there. Each male has an area of ground, called a territory, which he defends. In it, he and his mate will later build a nest and rear their young. Song thrushes start singing very early in February, when the fluting calls of the blackbird are also noticeable. If there is a mild spell, woodpeckers make their strange, drumming calls. They do this by banging their toughened beaks against tree trunks and branches.

Rooks and herons are gathering twigs as they set about repairing their large, untidy nests in the tree-tops. Winter bird migrants are still with us, including the huge flocks of starlings which fly to Britain from all over northern Europe. Great flocks of wood pigeons roam the country-side, often raiding farm crops in order to survive. Gulls swoop on town rubbish tips when the soil is too hard for them to be able to feed on farmland.

Many curious sea creatures, or their remains, are sometimes washed ashore during stormy weather at this time. There may be large squid, with their parrot-like beaks and long tentacles studded with suckers. Very often white cuttlefish bones are flung up by the tide, together with starfish, sea-squirts, razor-shells, crabs and large numbers of the shiny, black, purse-like egg-cases of skate. These break away from the seaweeds to which they were attached after the baby fish have hatched.

 song thrush   rook

 rabbit   heron

11

Making a bird nest box

Nest boxes not only provide the birds with somewhere to build their nests, they also act as warm, snug places for the birds to roost in winter. The box shown here, with a hole in the front, will attract blue tits, coal tits, great tits and other birds that normally nest in holes in tree trunks.

Along with an adult's help, you will need: a plank of wood 15cm wide x 142cm long, nails, a strip of rubber, catches.

Mark the wood as shown in the picture. Begin by cutting the wood into two pieces with an angled cut. Now make the other cuts so that you finish up with six pieces of wood.

Drill a hole in the front section.

If this is 29mm in diameter, the entrance hole will keep out house sparrows. Drill a few small holes in the floor section of the box. Then nail or screw the sections together.

Nail a strip of rubber to the lid and back to form a hinge. Fit a catch to each side of the lid.

Fix your nest box to a tree trunk, fence or wall, so that it is out of reach of cats and not in full sun. Nest boxes should be put up well before the nesting season begins, so that the birds have plenty of time to get used to them.

Don't touch the box during the nesting season but watch the birds from a safe distance. The hinged lid of the box is only for cleaning the old nest out in the autumn.

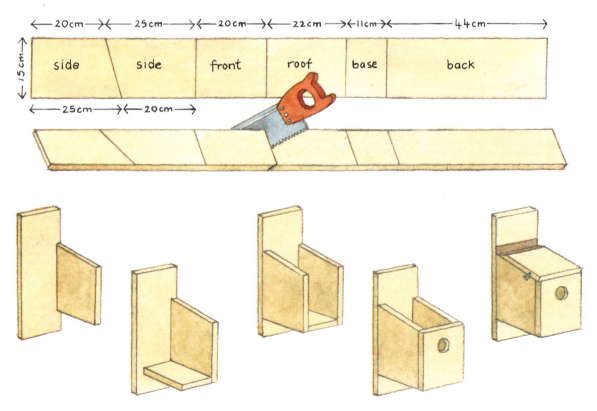

February

 chiffchaff pussy willow sparrow 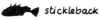 stickleback newt

March

March is the waking-up month for many butterflies that have spent the winter as adults. The first butterfly of the year is usually the brimstone. It has spent the winter outside, often hidden amongst the leaves of ivy and other evergreen shrubs and trees. Peacocks and small tortoiseshells have sheltered in buildings. On warm days these two butterfly species fly off in search of pussy willow and other early flowering plants. Pussy willow is also the main source of sweet food, or nectar, for moths that emerge in March from chrysalids or pupae. One is called the Earl Grey and is often to be seen resting on fences, posts, tree trunks and stone walls.

During this month the birds which have spent the winter in Britain will start to leave. But March also sees the arrival of the first of the migrating summer birds. One of the earliest to come is the chiffchaff, whose clear, piping song, chiff-chaff-chiff-chaff, can be heard until the end of June.

Many sorts of bird have already found a mate and set up a territory. But in order for mating to take place, some form of courtship is needed. Watch out for the male house sparrow hopping excitedly around his mate, with his tail raised and wings drooping. Later, the female crouches in front of the male, with drooping wings and twittering calls. Male pigeons court by puffing out their neck feathers while bowing and twisting in front of the females, who often continue feeding, pretending not to notice.

In fresh water, newts and stickle-backs also have elaborate courtships. The males develop special breeding colours. The male stickleback in particular shows a brilliant red throat during the breeding season. In open fields and heaths, hares too are courting at this time. As they court the females and chase rivals, male hares jump and kick and become the so-called 'mad March hares'.

Great masses of frogspawn can now be found in ponds and ditches. Each female common frog can lay up to 4,000 eggs at a time. A couple of weeks later, tadpoles wriggle free. Later this month toads will make their way to ponds and streams for spawning. They move at night; sometimes they have to cross roads and many die. At the water, each female lays a double string containing as many as 7,000 eggs.

hare

brimstone butterfly

brindled beauty moth

small tortoiseshell

A bird song diary

Bird species	J	F	M	A	M	J	J	A	S	O	N	D
blackbird												
chaffinch												
chiffchaff												
dunnock												
great tit												
greenfinch												
mistle thrush												
robin												
skylark												
song thrush												
wren												

It takes practice to be able to identify all the different bird songs. The easiest way to learn them is to go out with an experienced bird-watcher. If you can't do this, stick to the birds you know or can easily identify and record only those you actually see singing.

Keep a diary in your notebook of the birds you hear singing near your home or school. Each month, enter your findings in a chart like the one on this page.

Which bird species sings for the shortest time? Which sings longest? Are there any bird species which sing in every month of the year?

Rearing tadpoles

You will need: a small amount of frogspawn, an old, large, clean washing-up bowl, water plants, scraps of food, thread.

Collect your frogspawn from a pond or ditch. A dozen eggs is plenty. Put the frogspawn in the washing-up bowl with pond water and some water plants. Do not use tap water as this contains chemicals which may kill the eggs.

In your notebook, keep a diary in which you write down what happens to the eggs as they develop. How long do they take to hatch?

The baby tadpoles feed on plants at first. Later they will need animal food. Give them tiny pieces of raw meat or

16

chopped-up worms. Fix these to a piece of thread so that you can pull them out of the water after a few hours before they go bad.

As soon as the tadpoles have grown all four legs, put them back carefully in the pond or ditch where you took them from.

Bird song-posts

You will need: a sketching pad, a stick or piece of wood 1m long.

Many birds have a favourite spot from which they sing. It may be a bough of a tree, a clothes post, a chimney pot, a television aerial, a telegraph pole or a lamp-post.

Make a sketch-map of the song-posts of the birds in your garden, or in a small wood or park near your home.
Do different birds prefer certain types of song-post?

What height song-post does each species prefer? There are several ways of estimating the height of tall objects. One of the simplest is to stand your

stick or piece of wood in front of the object you want to measure. Stand some distance away and then estimate how many times the stick goes into the height of the tree, lamp-post or other object whose height you are trying to measure.

A butterfly diary

Year: 1996

Place:

Key: • seen occasionally   ✓ seen regularly   ✗ none seen

Name: | J | F | M | A | M | J | J | A | S | O | N | D

Red admiral
Peacock
Orange tip
Large white

Not all butterflies appear at the same time. You may find some indoors hibernating during the winter months. Others appear from chrysalids that formed in the previous autumn. A few butterflies may not be seen until well into July.

Make up a chart similar to the one shown and mark in the butterflies you see each day. The last butterfly species to appear will probably have migrated to this country from overseas.

Keep a record of the weather conditions when you see, or do not see, butterflies about. In which month do you see most butterflies?
What is the most common species?

Looking for bird rings

To find out about the journeys or migrations made by birds, bird-watchers attach a very light metal ring to the legs of some birds.

If you find a dead bird, look carefully to see if it has a ring on one of its legs. If it has, note the number on the ring and send it, with details of where and when you found the bird to the address which is stamped on the ring. If you do this, you will be helping scientists to find out more about the journeys birds make.

Always wash your hands thoroughly after touching a dead bird. Wear old gloves if you can.

18

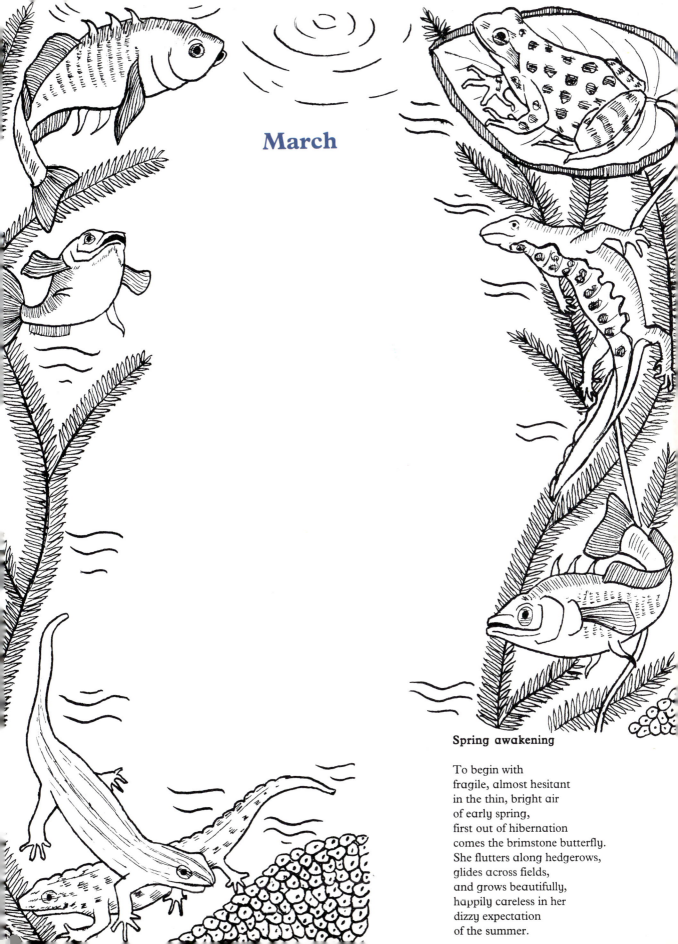

March

Spring awakening

To begin with
fragile, almost hesitant
in the thin, bright air
of early spring,
first out of hibernation
comes the brimstone butterfly.
She flutters along hedgerows,
glides across fields,
and grows beautifully,
happily careless in her
dizzy expectation
of the summer.

April

April is the time for nest-building. If the weather is wet, and there are plenty of earthworms about, blackbirds and thrushes are busy building their nests. The earthworms are food while mud from the wet ground is used to line the nests of both song-thrushes and blackbirds.

There are two ways in which birds bring up their young. Most young birds, such as blackbirds, thrushes, robins and chaffinches, are born blind and helpless. They stay in the nest until they are ready to fly. Usually, the nests of these birds are neat and tidy. Perhaps the most beautiful of all is that of the long-tailed tit, which is made largely of mosses and lichens and may be lined with over 1,000 tiny feathers.

Other birds, such as moorhens, mallard, pheasants and partridges have young which leave the nest

20

 long-tailed tit

 coot

 pheasant

 swallow   sandmartin

soon after hatching and usually feed themselves. The nests of these birds are generally untidy.

Small mammals, such as mice, voles and shrews, are also building nests. These are usually placed in underground burrows or other well hidden places. Few fishes make nests, apart from the stickleback. The brown trout, salmon and bullhead lay their eggs in holes and hollows in the gravel at the bottom of rivers and streams.

The weather also affects the arrival of summer bird visitors. Chiffchaffs, wheatears and sand-martins arrive at the end of March or beginning of April. Swallows and cuckoos come around the middle of the month.

After a shower of rain, slugs and snails appear to be everywhere. They feed on tender young plants and seedlings which grow rapidly in the warmer, moist conditions.

 shrew  wheatear cuckoo water vole wood mouse

21

A builder's yard for birds

You will need: nesting materials, a large string bag, string, sticks, an old, large tray.

At this time of the year, birds sometimes have difficulty in finding the right materials to build their nests with. You can help them by collecting together materials such as dry hay, dried moss, scraps of knitting wool cut into short pieces, the combings of dogs and cats, carpet fluff, sheep's wool and chicken feathers. Put them all into the bag. (One of the bags in which onions or Brussels sprouts come in are ideal for this.)

Hang the bag from a strong branch of a tree or from a clothes-line. Insert one or more sticks through the lower part of the bag to act as perches.

On the ground, near your net bag, put the tray. Fill it with wet mud.

Watch carefully to see which birds come to your builder's yard.
Which nesting materials do the birds seem to like best?

Warning: if there are birds nesting in your garden, do not go near the nest. The parents may leave their eggs or babies to die.

Mammals' nests

A good way of finding the underground nest of a small mammal, such as a mouse, vole or shrew, is to look under sheets of corrugated iron or large planks of wood which have been lying on the ground. Lift these objects quickly but carefully. Also lift any logs or large stones. Look at any nests you find – but don't touch them. Replace the 'lid' as you found it.

Homing snails

You will need: brightly coloured nail varnish.

Search under hedgerows, in old flowerpots, under planks and on rockeries for resting snails. With the nail varnish, mark their shells with a small number or letter. Mark the place where you found them in the same way. Move the snails a metre or two away. Check each day to see whether they have returned 'home'. Can you find any silvery slime trails to show which way the snails went? Do snails have a 'homing instinct' like that of racing pigeons?

Snails' teeth

You will need: a small basin, a spoon, flour and water, a clean jar, a hand lens.

You can easily watch a snail feeding. Mix a little flour with water to make a paste. Smear some of it on the inside of the jar and leave it to dry.

Put a snail inside the jar and let it crawl up the glass. Watch it feed on your paste. Look at it carefully with a hand lens. What are its teeth like? How many of them are there? How does the snail use its teeth to eat the paste?

Swallows return to the same nesting site every year.

Slug food preferences

You will need: an old margarine tub, kitchen paper, a selection of vegetables, a nail.

Line the bottom of the tub with several layers of dampened kitchen paper. Around the bottom of the tub arrange pieces of different plant materials. Try various wild plant leaves and pieces of lettuce, cabbage, a thin slice of raw carrot or potato, a piece of celery or onion, or any

other leaves or raw vegetables you can find.

Using a nail, make air-holes in the lid of the tub. Place a large slug in the box and put the lid on. Leave the box in a cool, dark place until the next day.

Look at the foods carefully. Which food did the slug like best? Try your experiment with different kinds of slugs. Do they all prefer the same kinds of foods?

Remember: let your slug go again where you caught it.

Sweeping for small animals

You will need: an old, wire coat-hanger, a plastic carrier bag, sticky tape, a hand lens.

Bend the coat-hanger into a diamond shape Take a plastic carrier bag and put one handle over the hook of the coat-hanger. Carefully tuck the bag opening over the wire diamond shape. Fix the top of the bag firmly in place with sticky tape.

Stinging nettles are growing rapidly now. Their leaves provide important food for lots of small animals. Gently swish your sweep bag to and fro through a clump of stinging nettles. After a few swishes look inside the net. How many small animals have you collected? What colour are they? Are they camouflaged? Look at your animals with a hand lens. Then set them free again where you caught them.

Use your sweep bag in long grass. Are the animals you find there different from those you found in the nettles? Sweep through dead or living tree leaves. What do you find there?

April

May

May brings long days with warm sunshine. Young birds are everywhere, but they shouldn't be touched. They haven't been abandoned but are sitting patiently waiting for their parents to come and feed them.

Life has begun to bubble up in ponds. Water snails glide along just below the surface, feeding on young duckweed plants. Whirligig beetles and pond skaters are looking for flies and other small insects.

Hedgerow flowers attract increasing hordes of bees, hoverflies, flying beetles, moths and butterflies. More and more spiders are building their webs, while tiny, scarlet mites run over the ground and baby bush-crickets sun themselves on young nettle leaves.

orange tip butterfly

large white butterfly

grass snake

red admiral

speckled wood butterfly

The warmer weather brings out reptiles. When a snake or lizard comes out of its hiding place in the morning, it can only move slowly. It finds a sunny spot to warm its body before it sets out to look for food.

Many species of mammal give birth to young this month including hedgehogs and squirrels. Fox cubs, born in late March or April, come out to play and learn to hunt, as do young badgers. Female rabbits may already be giving birth to their second or even third litter of the year, while in parks and forests red, fallow and roe deer are giving birth to dappled young. If you find a baby deer don't touch it; the mother deer will return to feed it when you are well out of the way.

fox   badger   pond skater   common lizard   whirligig beetle

Ants and food

You will need: tiny scraps of food, four or five clean milk bottle tops.

Find an ants' nest in your garden, playground, playing field or on a piece of waste ground.

Put a tiny piece of meat or biscuit in a milk bottle top near the nest. See how many ants come to the food. Do they pull the food to their nest? Now put down another piece of food twice as big as the first. Do twice as many ants arrive to pull it into the nest? To find out which food ants like best, place the milk bottle tops in a row near the ants' nest. Put a little jam in one, a little sugar in another, a little marmalade in another, a few biscuit or breadcrumbs in the next, and so on.

Watch carefully. Which bottle top do the ants go to first? Which is their favourite food? Do they take any of the foods back to their nest?

Making a formicarium

A formicarium is a home for ants.

You will need: a piece of glass or perspex about 16cm x 25cm, a piece of wood larger than the glass or perspex, Plasticine or modelling clay, a small rectangle of wood, an old container, plaster of Paris, a trowel, a large sheet of newspaper, a large jar with a cover made from a piece of an old pair of tights, cotton wool, honey or sugar, black card or cloth.

Lay the glass on the piece of wood. Build a wall of Plasticine or modelling clay around the edge of the glass. On top of it and within the wall of Plasticine, lay more pieces of Plasticine rolled out into long sausage shapes. Link these up with balls of Plasticine about the size of marbles. Join them in several different ways as shown in the picture. Near one end of the glass lay the small rectangle of wood. Join up one of the sausages of Plasticine to this.

Mix up some plaster of Paris with water. When the plaster is like thick cream, pour it into the mould you have made. Next day, when the plaster has dried, turn the cast over and remove the Plasticine and piece of wood. Clean up the glass and your formicarium is ready.

Have a look for an ants' nest in your garden or in a dry, sunny spot on a piece of waste ground or under logs or big stones. Use your trowel to dig around the nest in a circle about 60cm across. Remove the grass, if there is any, and try to follow the tunnels to the ant nest chambers, where most of the ants will be resting. Scoop up some soil containing ants, and place it in the centre of the sheet of newspaper. Remove any lumps and large stones, fold the paper in half then carefully shoot the contents into your jar and replace the cover. When you are digging, look carefully for the queen. She is usually larger and shinier than the other ants which are the workers. Try also to get a quantity of eggs, larvae and pupae and place them in the smaller pot.

Put the ants, eggs, larvae and pupae in the formicarium and replace the glass.

The ants will settle down quite quickly and move their eggs, pupae and larvae into separate chambers and begin to nurse them.

Place a little food in the rectangular chamber, together with the small piece of moistened cotton wool to provide water. Feed your ants with flies and other soft-bodied insects and a little honey or sugar solution. Feed them once a week and moisten the cotton wool whenever it dries.
Remove stale food and any dead ants regularly. Ants hate daylight in their nest, so keep the formicarium covered with a piece of black card or cloth when you are not looking at it.

After a month or two release the ants where you found them.
Clean the formicarium and then you could begin again with a new colony of ants.

Aggressive male sticklebacks

You will need: a large container with plenty of water plants, sand and shingle, a jam jar, a small mirror.

In the spring, male sticklebacks develop a bright red belly and throat and a dark blue back. They become very aggressive.

Catch a male stickleback in your jam jar. Put him in your container and leave him to settle down for a few hours. Put a small mirror in the container. Watch the stickleback attack his reflection, thinking it is another male.
Why do you think he doesn't attack female sticklebacks? How does he recognise them?

Insect visitors to flowers

You will need: coloured tissue paper, small sticks or pieces of wire.

Garden flowers come in all shapes, sizes and colours. Most of them rely on insects to carry pollen from one flower to another.

One way in which the harmless grass snake protects itself from its enemies is to pretend to be dead.

Spend 30 minutes or so carefully watching a flower-bed. In your notebook, keep a record of what kinds of insects visit the flowers. Say what colour flower each insect goes to. Do different kinds of insect have different coloured favourite flowers? To build up a really good record, repeat this activity several times each month throughout the summer.

Use coloured tissue paper to make some artificial flowers. Fix them to thin sticks or pieces of wire amongst real flowers. Do any insects visit your artificial flowers? Do more insects come if you paint a little sugar and water mixture in the middle of each artificial flower?

May

 frog

 tadpole

 green woodpecker

 spotted flycatcker

32

June

Long days and plenty of warm and sunny weather mean that June is the time of greatest activity for insects. Bees find fresh flowers to visit daily. Buzzing cockchafer beetles dash around the trees at night.

If the weather has been warm and dry, the tips of growing plants may be smothered with aphids – greenfly and blackfly. They suck the juices of the plant so much that the plant may wilt or even die. Fortunately, insect-eating birds, ladybirds, lacewings and the larvae of hoverflies prey on aphids and help to keep their numbers down.

Birds and mammals everywhere are working all through the daylight hours in search of food for their young families. Even in summer when food is more plentiful, it is still important to find as much as possible.

You can tell what sort of food a bird likes by looking at its beak and feet. Woodpeckers have chisel-shaped beaks for hammering through bark and wading birds have long, probing bills. Flesh-eating birds such as eagles, hawks and owls, have hook-shaped beaks for tearing the meat off their prey. Finches have strong, cone-shaped beaks for crushing seeds, while insect-eating birds have beaks like fine forceps.

In ponds and ditches wriggling swarms of tadpoles are growing fast in the warm sunshine. By the end of the month they will be tiny frogs or toads, hopping away at the first shower of rain – that is if they survive the attacks of hungry herons, water shrews, grass snakes and other enemies.

willow warbler

swift

lesser whitethroat

housemartin

Studying a pond

Pond-dipping can be very interesting and great fun. But you must **never** go looking for pond life alone. Always go with an adult and always push a stick into the water or mud to test the depth before you paddle at the edge.

You will need: an old pair of tights, a wire coat-hanger, a darning needle and strong thread, a stick, lots of jam jars, string, a white, plastic tray or old pie dish, a plastic spoon, a small paintbrush.

You can make your net by sewing a piece from one of the legs of the tights on to a frame made from bending the coat-hanger into a round shape and fixing it on to a stick. Tie the bottom tightly with string. Tie string around the tops of your jam jars so that they're easy to carry.

Approach the pond quietly to see what is moving about on, near or below the water. Carefully draw a sketch map of the pond in your notebook. Say how big it is and what the banks and bottom are like. What plants are growing round the edges?

Use your net carefully to search amongst the weeds for animals. Use it in clear water and over the surface of the bottom as well. After each sweep with your net, empty it out into the white tray. Use the plastic spoon and paintbrush to pick up small animals without damaging them.

Sort your catch into jars containing some pond water and a sprig of water weed. Only take one or two animals of each kind. Be careful to separate the fierce-looking carnivores in case they eat the other animals you have caught.

Pond animals

You will need: a hand lens, reference books.

Examine each of your pond animals in turn, using a hand lens.
Try to answer these questions about each animal.

How big is it?
What colour is it?
How many parts does it have to its body?
Does it have wings or wing covers?
What are its eyes like?
How many legs does it have? What are they like?

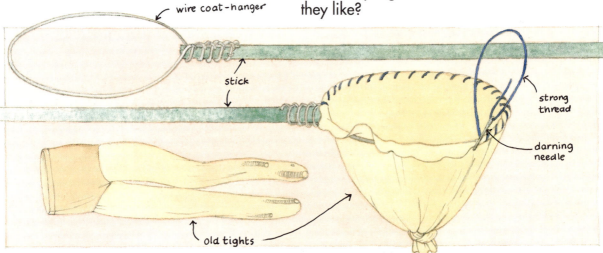

wire coat-hanger

stick

strong thread

darning needle

old tights

lens to study the snails' muscles as they climb up the glass. What do you notice? Watch how the snails feed. What kinds of foods do they eat?

Collect four or five more water snails. (If possible get different sizes and species.) Fill all the jars to the same level with pond water. Put one snail in each jar.

Watch the snails carefully for 30 minutes. How many times does each come to the surface for air? Do large snails make more visits to the surface than small snails?

Water snails' eggs

You will need: a white, plastic container, a hand lens.

Look carefully for water snails' eggs under the leaves of water lilies and other water plants. The eggs look like strips of jelly.

What does the animal eat?
How does it eat its food?
How does the animal breed?
Does the animal lay eggs, if so what do they hatch into?

Use reference books to find out the names of the animals. Be sure to put all your animals and plants back in the pond they came from when you have finished with them.

Water snails

You will need: a large jar, water plants, a hand lens, jam jars.

Put two or three water snails in a large jar of water with some water plants. Watch carefully to see how the animals move around inside the jar. Use a hand

Take a leaf which has eggs on it. Put it in a white dish together with some pond water. Study the eggs with a hand lens. How many eggs are there in one egg mass?

Keep the eggs in pond water. Use a hand lens to watch the baby snails develop. How many of them hatch out? What do the baby snails look like? How quickly do they grow?

Flatworms

You will need: a small piece of raw meat or liver, string, a white, plastic container, a hand lens.

Most ponds and ditches contain lots of flatworms. These tiny black or brown animals glide on the surface of water plants like pieces of ribbon.

A good way to collect some flatworms is to tie the piece of meat or liver to some string. Hang it in the water for about 15 minutes, then pull it out and look for flatworms sticking to it.

Fill your container with pond water, and put the flatworms into it. Watch them carefully as they swim around and feed on the meat or liver. Look at the flatworms with a hand lens. Can you see their eyes?

flatworm

leech

How leeches move

You will need: a white, plastic container, a hand lens.

Leeches are common pond animals. Put a leech into your container with some pond water. Look at the leech with a hand lens.

Draw a large picture of it in your notebook. Watch the leech to see how it moves. Draw a series of sketches to show how the animal uses its suckers.

Measure the leech when it is short and when it is stretched out. What is the difference between the two measurements?

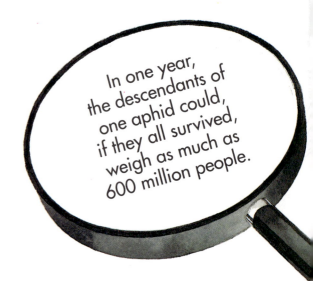

In one year, the descendants of one aphid could, if they all survived, weigh as much as 600 million people.

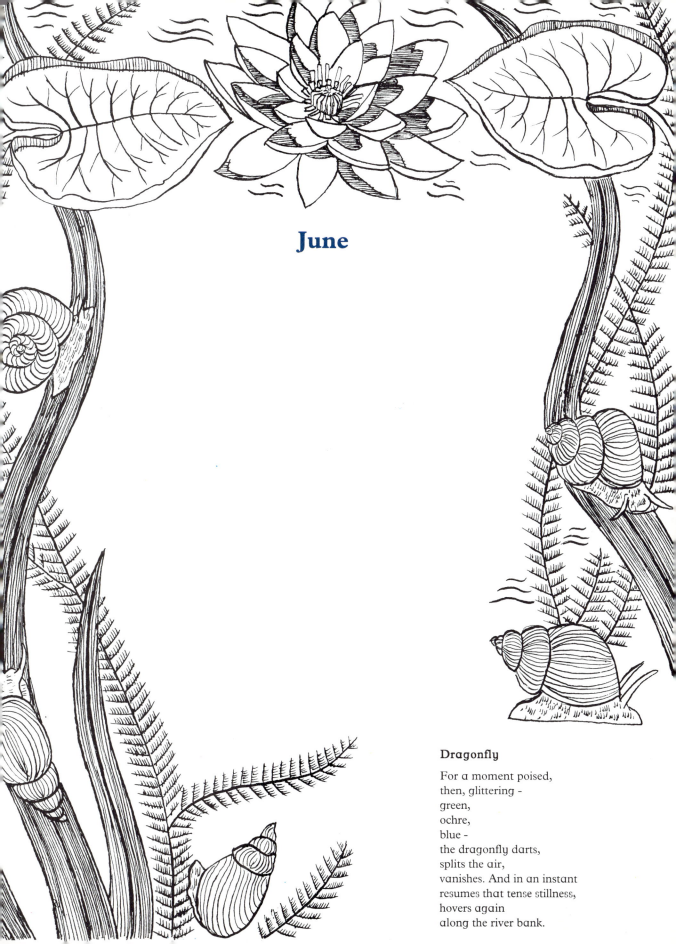

June

Dragonfly

For a moment poised,
then, glittering -
green,
ochre,
blue -
the dragonfly darts,
splits the air,
vanishes. And in an instant
resumes that tense stillness,
hovers again
along the river bank.

July

As this month progresses, the number of biting insects seems to increase and swarms of blood-sucking mosquitoes and midges are to be found near every river, lake, pond and marsh. Bee hives become crowded. Eventually, a large group of worker bees flies off with the old queen. The swarm soon settles on a branch and sends out scouts to look for a suitable nesting place. If the beekeeper doesn't catch the swarm quickly, it may form a new colony in the roof of a building or in a hollow tree.

Many birds have come to the end of their breeding season. The adult birds' feathers look worn and faded, while the plumage of many of the young birds makes it difficult to tell which species they belong to.

The young of many garden birds take only a week or two to grow up. By contrast, baby tawny owls stay with their parents for as long as three months so that they can learn and practise how to hunt. Tawny owls nest early, often in February or March, and the young start flying in late summer. Now is the time to listen at nights for their wheezing calls.

July is one of the best months of the year for bat watching. All the British species are out at dusk or at night, hunting for insects. With an adult, look for bats by woods and forests, near caves, large rubbish dumps (which attract insects) and water.

Young bats are born in June or July. The mother hangs with her

 magpie

 tawny owl

 collared dove

head up, and bends her tail forwards, making a pouch into which the young bat drops. It is born blind and naked and is fed by its mother on milk. The young bat clings to its mother for about a fortnight, even when she is flying.

The easiest of all night animals to watch are moths that settle on the outside of lighted windows.

These moths have been distracted from their search for nectar. They normally find their way using the light of the moon – something they learnt to do millions of years ago, long before light bulbs were invented. Unfortunately, moths have not learned to tell the difference between the moon and artificial light.

 house mouse

 bullfinch

 bat

 young robin

Gnats and mosquitoes

You will need: an old, large container, a hand lens.

Anyone can carry out this activity, wherever they live, because gnats and mosquitoes are common in the town and country.

Along with an adult, look for the eggs of gnats or mosquitoes (they are the same thing) on the surface of still water.
The eggs look like tiny rafts.
Good places to find them are in the water which collects in hollow trees, upturned dustbin lids, forgotten buckets, as well as ponds and ditches.

If you cannot find any eggs, put some pond water or the stale water from a vase of flowers into your container. Leave it outside for a week or two until gnats or mosquitoes have laid their eggs in it.

The eggs will hatch into tiny larvae or 'wrigglers' after a few days.
Each larva changes into a pupa after about three weeks. An adult gnat or mosquito develops inside the pupa and flies away after the skin of the pupa has split open.

Look at the various stages in the life history of the gnat or mosquito using a hand lens. Keep a record of what happens. Try to draw some of the stages.

Honey bee watching

Sit quietly near a flower which is being visited by honey bees. If you sit still and do not flap your arms you will not be stung.

Watch carefully to see the bee's long, tubular tongue unfolding. The bee is able to suck up nectar with its tongue just like someone sipping a drink through a straw.

The bee's body is covered with hairs. Notice how these sweep up the pollen from the flower's stamens. From time to time, the bee scrapes the pollen from the hairs with its legs. It puts it into baskets formed from curved hairs on its hind legs. Eventually, as the baskets fill, they look like little yellow lumps on the bee's hind legs.

Rearing caterpillars

You will need: an old, plastic sweet jar, a small bottle, some of the food plant on which you found the caterpillar, cotton wool, a plastic teaspoon, a small paintbrush, muslin, a rubber band.

the caterpillar changes into a pupa or chrysalis.

Keep the pupae in a cool place until the butterflies or moths emerge.
Let them go as soon as they start to fly.

Looking for animals at night

You will need: a torch, red tissue paper or cellophane, a rubber band.

Many animals that are active at night, such as mice, voles, badgers and foxes, cannot see red light.

Make your torch into a night-light for animal watching.
Cover the glass at the front with red tissue paper or cellophane. Hold it in place with the rubber band. The torch will now give out red light.

Fill the bottle with water and stand the food plant in it. Plug the neck of the bottle with cotton wool to stop the caterpillars falling into the water and drowning. Put this into the sweet jar.

Put two or three caterpillars on the food plant. Give them fresh food each day. Do not pick up the caterpillars with your fingers, but move them with a plastic teaspoon and a small paintbrush. Cover the top of the jar with muslin and hold it in place with the rubber band.

As a caterpillar grows, its old skin splits and there is a new, bigger one underneath. The last time this happens,

The light will be bright enough to show you the animals that are about, if you move quietly or, even better, keep completely still. But the light will not disturb the animals because they cannot see it.

Make sure that you always go with an adult when you are looking for animals at night-time.

41

Aphid births

You will need: a small bottle, cotton wool, an old, plastic sweet jar, a small paintbrush, cling-film, a rubber band, a hand lens.

Find a plant which has aphids (greenfly or blackfly) feeding on it. Pick a piece of the plant which doesn't have any aphids on it. A growing shoot is best.

Fill the bottle with water and put the leafy shoot into it. Plug the gap around the top of the bottle with cotton wool.

Stand the shoot and bottle in the sweet jar. Using your paintbrush, carefully move one aphid on to the leafy shoot. Cover the top of the jar with cling-film and hold it in place with the rubber band.

Watch the aphid carefully with a hand lens. Can you see it using its pointed mouthparts to suck the juices from the plant? Keep watching the aphid very closely. Before long it will give birth to a small baby aphid.

Make a regular count to see how many aphids you have in your jar. How many aphids are there after a day... three days... a week?

Put a ladybird in the jar with your aphids. Watch how it catches and eats them. How many aphids does a ladybird eat in a day? Does a ladybird eat all of each aphid? If not, what does it do with the leftovers?

Collecting feathers

You will need: a hand lens, a sheet of card, sticky tape.

Collect feathers from gardens, parks, woods and fields. Look at them with a hand lens to see how they are made up. The flat part of the feather is called the vane. Run it between your fingers and you will see that it is formed of minute hooked branches which fit neatly together.

Fix the feathers into your notebook or on a sheet of card using sticky tape. Label each with the bird's name and where and when you found it.

An owl can turn its head through 180 degrees and look directly behind it.

42

July

August

August is the time when people go on their summer holidays, with many going to the seaside.

Generally, animals on a sandy shore are hidden below the surface. However, if you lift one of the heaps of rotting seaweed washed up by the tide, you will probably find that sandhoppers leap away in all directions. The tellin and edible cockle hide just below the surface of the wet sand, as does the razor-shell. You will have to dig carefully if you want to find them.

Rocky shores with scattered rock pools are the most exciting habitats at the seaside. Hidden amongst the seaweeds growing in

 pipefish
 shore crab
 lobster
 oystercatcher ter

44

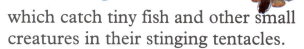

which catch tiny fish and other small creatures in their stinging tentacles.

Limpets are large, cone-shaped shells which hold tight to the rocks. When the tide comes in, they move around, feeding on tiny plants called algae which grow on the rocks.

Among the snail-like animals with a single shell are periwinkles, edible winkles and dog whelks. The double-shelled animals (called bivalves) will almost certainly include mussels. These animals feed by drawing in water and filtering tiny bits of food from it. Some small fish may remain in rock pools after the tide has gone out. Those you are most likely to see are common blennies, rock gobies and pipefish.

It's worthwhile having a look at sand-dunes or grassy cliffs behind the shore. On the south and west coasts of Britain at this time of year, hundreds of migrant insects arrive from overseas. They include the painted lady, red admiral and clouded yellow butterflies, hummingbird hawk moths, hoverflies and dragonflies. Many of the seabirds are still busy nesting and rearing their young at the beginning of this month, so on quiet beaches keep a look out for camouflaged baby gulls, terns, oyster-catchers and other birds.

these pools you may find many animals, including crabs or even a lobster, all with their heavy armour of shell. Prawns and shrimps dart from stone to stone and hermit crabs make their homes in old whelk shells or large periwinkles. Attached to the rocky sides of the pool you may find sea anemones – flower-like animals

 cockle  razor shell limpet  whelk  prawn

45

Exploring a rock pool

You will need: a net.

Sit quietly by a rock pool. Try not to let your shadow fall over the water. Wait for the animals to come out and behave as if you were not there.

You could search the pool with a net. Turn stones and sift through the seaweeds to see what is hiding there. Remember to replace everything as you found it when you have finished.

A rock pool viewer

You will need: a large ice-cream container, cling-film, a large rubber band.

Have you ever wished you could look underwater in a rock pool and see clearly what is there?

Cut the bottom from the container and stretch cling-film over it. Hold the cling-film firmly in place with the rubber band.

Gently push the bottom of the container into the rock pool.
Look through it and watch what is happening under the water. Use your viewer only in small rock pools.

Watching barnacles

You will need: a jar, a drinking straw, some cold soup or gravy.

Search rock pools for some barnacles on a small stone. Put the stone into the jar filled with sea-water.

Watch carefully and you will see the barnacles open their shells and put out their feathery limbs which they wave to catch bits of food in the water.

Use a drinking straw to put two or three drops of cold gravy or soup in the water. What do the barnacles do?

After the experiment, return the barnacles to the place where you found them.

Fishing for crabs

You will need: a small piece of raw meat or fish, string.

Crabs will often eat a piece of raw meat or fish, so this is a good way of luring them out of their hiding places.

Tie the piece of meat or fish to the end of a thin piece of string. Dangle it in a large rock pool near rocks where a crab may be hiding.

If a crab comes out to investigate it may grab the food in its claws. If it holds on tightly you can pull it out.

Look at the crab carefully – particularly at its eyes and mouthparts. Count how many legs it has. Watch it walk across the beach. What do you notice about the way it walks? Let the crab go back into the rock pool it came from.

Feeding a cockle

You will need: a jam jar, a drinking straw, some cold soup or gravy.

Half fill a jam jar with sand, then fill the remainder with sea-water.

Put a cockle into the jar. When the water clears you will see the cockle's two breathing tubes, or siphons, sticking up above the sand.

Use a drinking straw to put two or three drops of gravy or soup just above the cockle. Watch the cockle suck the food in a stream into one of its siphons.

Painting limpets

You will need: bright nail varnish, kitchen towel.

Look for limpets at low tide. Mark four or five of them with blobs of nail varnish. Put similar marks on the rocks nearby. You may need to dry a small area of the limpet shell and the rock to be certain that the varnish dries. Use a paper towel for this.

Look at where the limpets are the next day. Have any of them moved? How can you tell?

Collecting shells

You will need: a smallish, soft brush, kitchen paper, matchbox trays or a shoebox lid, cotton wool, lubricating oil.

It's interesting to make a collection of sea shells. Collect only empty shells. Clean them in tap water and brush off any mud or sand with your brush.

Dry the shells with the kitchen paper and store them in the matchbox trays or shoebox lids lined with cotton wool. The shells will keep for always like this. Label each shell with the name of the animal that it belonged to and where and when you found it.

If you want your shells to have a 'wet' look, rub them lightly with a little of the oil.

You can also collect snail shells in the same way, but again, only ever collect empty shells.

August

September

If the weather is warm and sunny, insects and spiders seem to be everywhere. In parks and gardens, butterflies swarm on the flowers of buddleia, ice-plant and Michaelmas daisies. As the month progresses, they turn their attentions to ripe blackberries, apples and other seasonal fruits. They are accompanied by greenbottle and bluebottle flies, hoverflies and great crowds of worker wasps. The latter have not been very noticeable throughout the summer, as they have been collecting flies and other harmful insects to feed their larvae. Now the larvae are fully-grown wasps, so the workers have no more work to do. As a result they turn to fruits and other sweet foods, and become a major pest to humans.

 treecreeper bluebottle greenbottle wasp

The many insects are preyed upon by spiders, whose webs can easily be seen as they glisten in the early morning mists. Hammock-shaped webs are the work of money-spiders. They hang beneath their webs, waiting to pounce on any unfortunate insect which becomes trapped. The garden spider builds an orb web. This is a wheel of sticky threads which can trap insects as large as a wasp. The spider lurks at the centre, running out along specially dry threads to catch and kill its victim.

Birds, too, are feeding on the many insects and other small animals. It is at this time of the year that you often notice thrushes' anvils. These are stones, bricks or pieces of concrete on which song thrushes break the shells of snails they have caught in the area.

In large parks, forests and areas of moorland, it is the rutting season of red and fallow deer. The males fight each other to claim the biggest territory with the most females in it.

 orb web

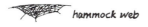 hammock web

 five-band snail

 hoverfly

Marble galls on oak trees

You will need: jam jars, cling-film,
a rubber band, a hand lens, a small,
sharp knife.

Marble galls are caused by small,
brown, ant-like insects called gall
wasps. They lay their eggs inside oak
tree twigs. At first the galls are green,
then they turn brown in September.

Put a few marble galls in a jar.
Cover it with cling-film and prick
a few tiny air-holes in it. Hold the
cling-film in place with a rubber
band. Look at the galls every day.
Watch for the tiny gall wasps to come
out in the autumn. Look at them with
a hand lens. How did they get out of
the gall?

Carefully cut a gall in half after the
wasp has left it. Can you see the tiny
chamber where the gall wasp lived
and grew?

Examine an oak tree carefully for
other kinds of galls, such as oak apples
and spangle galls. Keep some of them in
jars. What kinds of small animals
come out of them?

Thrushes' anvils

You will need: Plasticine.

Keep a look out for a thrush's anvil.
This is the large stone or piece of
brick or concrete on which the thrush
breaks open snail shells.

Look at the shells carefully. Most of
them will probably be banded snails.
These come in several different colours.

Which colour snail does your thrush find most of? Which colour does it find least of?

Watch your thrush's anvil carefully from a distance. (You could use binoculars if you have some.) Exactly how does the thrush open the snail shell and eat the snail?

Song thrushes often take empty snail shells to their 'anvils' and leave them unbroken. They never seem to realise that the shells are lighter than usual. Pack empty snail shells with different amounts of Plasticine and leave them in a place on the lawn or a pathway where the birds will easily see them.

How do the thrushes react to these artificial snails? If a snail shell is too heavy for the thrush to carry, what does it do?

Robins' pincushions

You will need: a small, sharp knife.

Look at wild rose plants this month. They often have red, fluffy balls on them that look like red moss. These are called robins' pincushions. They develop when a tiny insect lays its eggs in the stems or leaves of the rose plant.

Carefully cut open a robin's pincushion. Can you see the little grubs which have hatched from each egg?

Some caterpillars look like bird droppings in order to deceive their enemies.

Keeping spiders

You will need: a large, plastic sweet jar or container, soil, the inside of a toilet roll or matchbox, a branched twig, a small dish or lid, cling-film, a rubber band, a hand lens.

Spiders can be found almost everywhere. Here is a way to make a home for one so that you can observe it for a little while. Only keep one spider in your container, since they are carnivores and will even eat each other.

Put a layer of damp soil in the bottom of the container. Give the spider the cardboard roll or a partly open matchbox to hide in. If there is room, add the twig so that the spider can build a web. Make a few air-holes in the cling-film and cover the jar with it; hold the cling-film in place with the rubber band.

Give your spider a small dish or lid of water to drink. Feed it on flies or other small insects. Watch carefully to see how it kills its prey. Are there any parts of the food which are not eaten? What does the spider do with these?

If your spider builds a web, draw the different stages of web-building.

What happens if you touch the finished web with a blade of grass? Look at the web with a hand lens. What makes the web sticky? If you make a small hole in the web, does the spider repair it or does it make a completely new web?

Let your spider go again where it came from after a week or so. You could always catch another spider of a different species and see if that behaves in exactly the same way as your first one.

Collecting spiders' webs

You will need: a piece of black card, scissors, glue, cling-film.

Cut a piece of card slightly larger than the web you want to collect.

Put a few tiny spots of glue around the edge of the piece of card. Gently lift the card towards the web from behind until it sticks. Cut the silken threads outside the card. When the glue is dry, cover the web with cling-film to protect it.

Label each web, saying where and when you collected it and, if you can, what kind of spider made it.

September

Unseen drama

As a thousand insects entangle themselves
in a scaffold of threads;
As a thousand money spiders hang
beneath the hammocked webs
and wait to pounce;
I sigh,
my senses aware only of
the shards of glistening gossamer
that coat the early morning misted grass.

October

As winter approaches, the days get shorter and the weather becomes colder and wetter. Food for animals is getting scarcer, particularly for those that feed mainly on insects. Swallows, martins, cuckoos and warblers are among the birds that avoid the cold and lack of food by migrating south to warmer climates.

Many trees and shrubs are covered with brightly coloured fruits. Flocks of starlings and pigeons feed on these.

Tits, finches, mice and voles are gathering mast (which is what the hard seeds of the beech tree are called). Jays, pigeons, pheasants, rooks and squirrels are among the many animals feasting on acorns. Squirrels are hoarders of acorns, hazel nuts and sweet chestnuts at this time of the year. Wood mice store nuts and berries in old birds' nests and hollow trees, as well as having underground food stores near to their nest chambers.

This month the yellowish-green flowers of ivy open. They are not particularly bright and you might not even notice them, but insects find them very attractive. On fine days they are visited by wasps, hoverflies and small tortoiseshell and red admiral butterflies. If you search carefully among the ivy leaves and branches, you may find caterpillars of the pale yellow swallow-tailed moth.

October is the time when earwigs retreat into crevices in the soil for the winter. The female lays a small cluster of eggs, often in a

 greenfinch

 chaffinch

 rook

hollow under a stone. Like a broody hen she then covers them with her body, keeping them together and cleaning them from time to time. When eggs hatch in the spring the female still feeds and looks after the babies until they are big enough to fend for themselves.

 wood mouse

 jay

 squirrel

interesting bits. Look for the skulls of birds and mammals and the wing cases of beetles.

Mount the contents of one of the pellets on a piece of card. Say which bird made the pellet and where and when you collected it. Label the parts of the pellet if you can.

Always wash your hands thoroughly after touching bird pellets.

Bird pellets

You will need: old gloves, several jam jars, an old, shallow dish, tweezers, a darning needle, a piece of card.

Birds of prey such as eagles, hawks and owls eat small animals whole. They then get rid of the parts they cannot digest by coughing them up in a pellet. Many other birds including rooks, crows, herons, robins and flycatchers also do this.

You can find these pellets if you search under the bird's favourite roosting place. Make sure you are wearing your gloves and collect some of the pellets. They do not smell. Soak the pellets individually in jars of water for several hours. Put the remains in a shallow dish. Use your tweezers and needle to help you to pick out the

A Tullgren funnel

You will need: a jam jar, kitchen paper, black paper, a large funnel, rotting tree leaves, a desk lamp, a hand lens, a reference book.

Many tiny animals live in rotting leaf litter. You can collect some of them if you make a Tullgren funnel.

Line the jam jar with damp kitchen towels. Cover the outside with black paper. Stand the funnel in the top of the jar. Fill the funnel with a handful of leaves.

Ask a grown-up to arrange the desk lamp for you. See that the light goes straight down to the top of the leaves. This type of funnel works because the small animals move away from the heat and light of the lamp and fall into the jar below. Examine the animals with a hand lens and try to identify them using a reference book. Let them go again in some more rotting leaves when you have finished looking at them.

Birds on the water

You will need: a stop-watch or watch with a second hand.

Watch the birds on your local lake. Which birds feed by 'dabbling'? (This means the bird runs its beak along the surface of the water by rapidly opening and closing it while straining food out of the water.) Some birds put their heads under water, which makes them look as though they are standing on their heads while feeding. Can you see any of these? Other water birds dive under water completely to feed. Which species are they?

Using your watch, you can make a study of diving birds. Each time, say, a great-crested grebe goes under water, time how long its dive lasts. Do this several times for each bird of each species. If you can, work out an average for each bird species.

Which species has the longest average dive? Which has the shortest dive?

Birds and berries

There are many kinds of berries ripening on trees and shrubs in gardens, parks and hedgerows at this time. Choose a tree or shrub with lots of bright berries and see which kinds of birds come to eat them.

Keep a record of the birds you actually see eating the berries (not those that may just be resting on the tree or bush). Make a note of what the weather was like. Then move on to watch a different kind of tree or shrub which has berries.

Eventually, you will be able to say which bird species prefer which kinds of berries. What is the weather like when birds eat most berries?

Making a slug or snail home

You will need: a large, plastic sweet jar, a clump of grass, soil, a large stone or piece of bark, scraps of lettuce, cabbage, or stinging nettles, cling-film, a rubber band, a plastic spoon, a hand lens, a jar, a piece of black paper.

Put a layer of moist soil in the bottom of your container and lay the stone or piece of bark and the grass on top. Put two or three slugs or snails in the container. Give them lettuce, cabbage or stinging nettles to eat. Make some small air-holes in the cling-film and cover the jar. Hold the cling-film in place with the rubber band. Always remove any stale food quickly.

Slugs and snails lay small, white eggs in the soil. If you find any, pick them up carefully with the spoon. Look at them with your hand lens. Can you see the tiny animals growing inside the egg?

Put the eggs in a separate jar of moist soil. How long do they take to hatch? What does a baby slug or snail look like?

Place one of your slugs or snails on a piece of black paper. Watch it crawl across. Can you see the slime trail it leaves? This slime trail helps the slug or snail to crawl more easily.

October

November

Increasing numbers of bird travellers from the north are making the dangerous sea crossing by day and night to reach Britain and other places further south. People who live near the coast will hear thousands of redwings, fieldfares and blackbirds, as well as ducks, geese and swans, calling in the fog as they try to keep in touch with each other. Soon these birds will spread inland to feed on hedgerow berries and fruits.

At this time of the year there seem to be flocks of birds everywhere. Chaffinches, greenfinches and bramblings join the flocks of sparrows feeding on farmland. Linnets, snow buntings and shore larks haunt the coast where seeds are washed up by the tides. Inland, gulls follow the farmer's plough, joining the lapwings, jackdaws and rooks digging for worms and insect grubs on the fields by day. Starlings and pigeons form their own separate feeding flocks. At night, many of these species collect in even larger flocks to roost.

 brambling

 greenfinch

 linnet

 skylark

As the cold weather sets in, hedgehogs are settling down to sleep in their leafy nests beneath the tree roots, in piles of rubbish or even in unlit bonfires. Newts have crept into cellars and under logs and stones.

But where have all the insects gone? Some, such as ladybirds, queen wasps, queen bumble bees and a few species of butterfly manage to survive the winter as adults, by hibernating in places such as inside hollow trees, under bark, in dense ivy or in buildings. Others have solved the problem of the cold in a different way. The adults lay their eggs before winter sets in – and then die. It is the eggs, larvae or pupae that will survive over the winter. This large group includes the vast majority of butterflies and moths, aphids and grasshoppers.

swan   jackdaw   lapwing   barnacle geese

Making a wormery

You will need: a large, plastic jar, soil, sand or peat, two or three dead tree leaves, an old pair of tights, a rubber band, black paper.

Put a layer of moist soil, about 3cm thick, into your jar. Follow this by a thin layer of either sand or peat. Then put another layer of moist soil, then a thin layer of sand or peat and so on until the jar is almost full.

Place three or four earthworms on to the soil. Lay the leaves on the surface of the soil. Keep the soil moist but not very wet. Cover the top of the jar with a piece cut from the tights and hold it in place with the rubber band. Cover the outside of the jar with a piece of black paper. Keep the wormery in a cool place.

After a week, take off the paper. Look at what the worms have done to the layers of soil. What has happened to the leaves you left on top of the jar?

What are the earthworms' burrows like? Can you see any little heaps of soil which the worms have passed through their bodies? These are called worm casts.

Collecting birds' nests

You will need: old gloves, plastic bags, insect powder (one containing pyrethrum is best), rubber bands, shoeboxes.

Most birds build new nests each year, so you can safely collect old nests in the autumn when the birds have finished with them.

Collect the nests in dry weather. Then, wearing gloves, dust them with a little of the insect powder and carefully put each nest in a plastic bag. Secure the bag with a rubber band and leave it for a day or so. Any fleas or lice in the nests will die.

Pull one of the nests to pieces carefully to see what it is made of. If you have room, you can display your nests, in a shoebox, for example.

Label each nest with the name of the kind of bird which made it and where and when you found it.

November

 pheasant
 hare
 fallow doe
 fallow b

December

You may not feel much like going out on cold December evenings, but if you do you may be surprised at how many animals are still active. There are, for example, a number of moth species still alive, including the winter moth, the scarce umber, the spring usher and the pale brindled beauty. The most unusual thing about these moths is that the females are small and wingless.

Although snails are safely tucked up inside their shells until mild weather returns, unless the weather is very cold and windy or there is deep snow on the ground, their relatives, the slugs, are still active. Throughout the winter, inside the warmth of rotting logs, compost heaps and layers of decaying tree leaves, a whole variety of insect larvae and other small animals is thriving.

Berries of privet, yew, holly, juniper and mistletoe, not only provide attractive Christmas decorations, they are also important foods for birds in December. Blackbirds, fieldfares, redwings and pheasants feed upon the berries and, occasionally, beautiful waxwings from Scandinavia arrive to feed when the berry crop in their own country has failed.

Although they are probably no easier to see in winter than in summer, you can often see where mammals have been by the signs they leave behind. Most mammals, from deer to mice, for example, use regular paths, and these tend to show up more clearly in winter, particularly if there is snow or heavy frost on the ground. In hard weather, mice, voles, rabbits, hares, squirrels and deer will all strip the bark from trees when other foods are scarce. Squirrels will use tree stumps as tables on which to eat pine cones or hazel nuts. Burrows and nests show up more clearly at this time, as do footprints, droppings, discarded fur or feathers.

 fieldfare

 redwing

 waxwing

A pitfall trap

You will need: a plastic jar, two stones, a piece of wood or slate, a hand lens, a reference book, scraps of food.

This simple trap will catch many of the animals that scurry across your garden at night.

Sink the plastic jar into the ground until its rim is level with the ground. Put a stone either side of the top and cover it with the piece of wood or slate to keep out the rain.

Empty the trap in the morning. Look at the animals you have caught with a hand lens. Use reference books to identify them.

Set more traps in different parts of the garden. What happens if you put little pieces of bait in the traps, such as breadcrumbs, meat, cheese or ripe fruit?

Let the animals go and always remove your traps when you have finished with them, otherwise you will kill many small animals which will fall into them and be unable to get out.

Life in a rotting log

You will need: a torch, a plastic bag, newspaper, a jam jar, a plastic spoon, a small paintbrush, a hand lens.

A fallen tree branch or trunk provides a home for many different animals as it rots away.

If there is a rotting log near your home, go out with an adult and use a torch to look at it carefully after dark. Peep under the bark. What small animals can you see? If the log is not too big, look underneath it. What small animals are living there? Remember to put the log back exactly as it was, otherwise you will be destroying the hiding place of many small animals.

If the log is really small you could take it home. Gently put it inside a plastic bag. When you get home, cover a table with sheets of newspaper.

Lay the log on the paper and carefully take it to pieces. Keep a record of all the small animals you find. As you find each small animal, gently pick it up by pushing it on the plastic spoon with the help of the paintbrush.

Look at the animals you have collected with a hand lens. Which kind was the most common in your rotting log? Let the animals go near some more rotting logs when you have finished studying them.

December

Today I saw a crow
Drinking in are bird Bath
for the first time.

Freeze-frame

W hilst hedgehog sleeps
I cicles form. Giant's jewels
N ecklace the fence around the lake.
T all heads of reedmace wither, furry brown, and
E ven the pike lies low,
R emote and still.

Glossary

Aggressive: likely to attack first, attacking first

Aphid: a tiny insect, often called a greenfly or blackfly, that sucks sap from plants

Artificial: made by people, not by nature

Bait: food which is put on a hook or in a trap to catch fish or other animals

Camouflage: to disguise the appearance of something or someone; a way of hiding people or things so that they look like their surroundings

Carnivore: an animal that eats meat

Caterpillar: a long, creeping creature (a larva) that turns into a butterfly or moth

Chrysalis: the resting stage or pupa into which a caterpillar changes before it becomes a butterfly or moth

Colony: a group of people, birds or other animals living together

Court: to try to win someone's love or support

Estimate: to guess, to calculate approximately

Fertilise: to make fertile; to make able to produce young

Formicarium: an artificial home for ants

Herbivore: an animal that eats plants

Homing: trained to fly home, like a homing pigeon

Insect: any of a group of animals with a hard outer skeleton and a body divided into three parts. Insects have three pairs of legs and most have two pairs of wings

Instinct: a natural tendency to behave in a certain way

Invertebrate: an animal without an internal skeleton or backbone

Larva: a part of the life cycle of insects and other animals without backbones. The larva hatches from an egg and has a soft, wormlike body. The caterpillars of butterflies and moths and the maggots of flies are larvae

Maggot: the larva of some kinds of fly

Mammal: a vertebrate animal the female of which can feed her young with her own milk

Migration: to go to live in another country or another part of the country

Migrant: a migrating animal or person

Navigate: to direct and control the course of a ship, aircraft, person or animal

Nectar: a sweet liquid collected by bees and other insects from flowers

Nymph: one of the stages in the development of some insects, such as dragonflies, before they become adults

Pollen: the yellow powder or dust made by the stamens of flowers

Pupa: one of the stages in the life cycle of insects such as butterflies, moths and flies. The pupa of a butterfly or moth is often called a chrysalis

Queen: the egg-laying female of insects such as ants, bees and wasps

Reptile: a cold-blooded animal with a scaly skin which creeps or crawls. Snakes, lizards and tortoises are reptiles

Solitary: alone, lonely, one only

Spawn: the eggs of fish, frogs, toads or newts which are laid in water

Specialise: to give particular attention to one thing or subject. To be a specialist or expert in a particular subject

Specimen: one of a group used as an example of the rest of the group

Stamen: the male part of a flower which produces pollen

Temperature: the amount of heat or cold in something

Temporary: for a short time only

Tentacle: one of the long, finger-like organs found on the heads of some invertebrate animals

Territory: an area of land in which an animal or group of animals lives. Other animals entering the territory are attacked, particularly in the breeding season

Thermometer: an instrument for measuring temperature

Vertebrate: an animal with an internal skeleton and a backbone

Useful books

Birdfeeder Handbook
Robert Burton (*Dorling Kindersley*)

**Clue Books: Freshwater Animals   Insects
Birds, Tracks and Signs**
Gwen Allen and Joan Denslow (*Oxford University
Press*)

Discovering Animals
Tony Soper (*Guild Publishing*)

**Discovering Nature: Slugs and Snails
Squirrels   Birds of Prey   Rats and Mice
Rabbits and Hares   Badgers   Snakes and
Lizards** (*Wayland*)

**The Eyewitness Guides: Bird   Pond and River
Butterfly and Moth   Mammal   Shell
Seashore   Fish   Woodland**
(*Dorling Kindersley*)

How to Look at Wildlife
Bob Gibbons (*Hamlyn*)

The Kestrel in the Town
Mike Birkhead (*Methuen*)

The Ladybird Book of British Birds
Robert Dougall

The Life Cycle of a Snail
Jennifer Coldrey (*Wayland*)

Life in Fresh Water
Ed Catherall (*Wayland*)

The Squirrel in the Trees
Jennifer Coldrey (*Methuen*)

The Sunday Times Countryside Companion
Geoffrey Young (*Country Life Books*)

Things to See and Do in the Garden
Michael Chinery (*Granada*)

A Walk Through the Seasons
Alfred Leutscher (*Methuen*)

The Young Naturalist
Andrew Mitchell (*Usborne*)

**The Young Scientist Investigates: Small
Garden Animals   Birds   Sea and Seashore
Rocks and Soil   Pond Life**
Terry Jennings (*Oxford University Press*)

The Zoo in the Town David Taylor (*Boxtree*)

The Zoo in the Garden David Taylor (*Boxtree*)

Useful addresses

**Royal Society for the Prevention of
Cruelty to Animals (RSPCA)**
Junior Membership
Causeway
Horsham
West Sussex RH12 1HG

Watch
The Green
Witham Park
Waterside South
Lincoln LN5 7JR

Watch Scotland
Scottish Wildlife Trust
5 Calton Hill
Edinburgh EH1 3BJ

Worldwide Fund for Nature UK (WWF)
Panda House
Weyside Park
Godalming
Surrey GU7 1XR

**Young Ornithologists' Club (YOC),
c/o Royal Society for the
Protection of Birds (RSPB)**
The Lodge
Sandy
Bedfordshire SG19 2DL

**The Young People's Trust for
Endangered Species**
95 Woodbridge Road
Guildford
Surrey GU1 4BB

First published 1991
by Charles Letts & Co Ltd
Diary House, Borough Road,
London SE1 1DW

Text: © Terry Jennings 1991

Poems: © Irene Yates

Illustrations: Ann Winterbotham, Judy Stevens

© Charles Letts & Co Ltd 1991

Cover illustration: Julie Douglas

Editorial team: Mary-Jane Wilkins, Karen Sparrock

Design team: Anne Davison, Keith Anderson

ISBN 0 85097 924 2

Printed and bound in Italy

Inspired by the Memoirs of

Olaudah Equiano

Preface

The islanders of Guadeloupe, in the Caribbean, planned many projects to commemorate the year slavery was abolished. In the library at Pointe-à-Pitre there was a large collection of writings about slavery. The librarians put together a catalogue of these works, which was made available on the town's website.

Buried in this list of writings was one special book – an autobiography, translated into French and published in 1987 by Caribbean publishers. This was an original work written by a freed and literate slave.

The librarians very quickly saw that they had in their hands an amazing account of this slave's tragic exodus out of Africa: the terrible sea voyage, his experiences as a slave at the hands of his masters, and his liberation.

But although it was the librarians who unearthed these pages and restored them, it is the illustrator who gave a face to Equiano, our hero. The librarians and the Book Salon asked Jean-Jacques Vayssières, a Caribbean artist, to mount an exhibition illustrating this extraordinary story. In 1998, the visitors to the Guadeloupe Book Fair were able to view, in pictures, the stormy and brave adventures of the young slave.

As he painted the life of Equiano, Jean-Jacques Vayssières became captivated by the personality and the unique experiences of the young slave. Equiano became an ever-present character in Jean-Jacques' daily life, and was never far from his thoughts. Convinced that he should share this new friendship with young people in particular, Jean-Jacques decided to bring Equiano to life in this story.

Written and Illustrated by
Jean-Jacques Vayssières

The Amazing Adventures of
Equiano

IAN RANDLE PUBLISHERS–*Jamaica*
LANTERN BOOKS–*Nigeria*
NEW AFRICA BOOKS–*South Africa*
SAM-WOODE LTD–*Ghana*

Le porteur de ce billet
Gustave Vasa, a été
mon esclave pendant
plus de trois ans,
période pendant laquelle
il s'est toujours bien
conduit, accomplissant
sa tâche avec honnêteté
et application
Robert King

Montserrat, 26 janvier 1767

4

The good-looking young man paused, with one foot on the gangway. He read the words written by Robert King again.

The bearer of this letter was my slave for more than three years. He always behaved well, carrying out his tasks both seriously and honestly.

> *Robert King*
> *Montserrat*
> *January 26, 1767*

He could not believe it! He was finally free – his life as a slave was over. Not far from him, the sight of a terrified child suddenly reminded him of himself at the same age, ten years earlier in Barbados. He shook off the thought.

'I'm twenty years old now. And free!'

This story begins in 1756, when Equiano, our hero, is ten years old. He was born into the Ibo tribe, in the rich valley of Isseke, on the border of the powerful African Kingdom of Benin. The Ibo were hard-working people – and famous for their excellent dancers and musicians. They were faithful to their customs, but were also open to new ideas.

The Talented Slave

Breathing hard, shaking with effort, and spurred on by the shouting crowd, Equiano threw his rival to the ground.

'Aieee!' He had lived up to his name.

Olaudah meant 'good luck' in the Ibo language, and his good luck had just won him the wrestling match. He was bursting with pride. He was also proud that he had won this match because he knew that his father had been watching him, even though he seemed to be deep in conversation with the Council Elders of the tribe.

8

In the background, bursts of laughter and the pounding of pestles in wooden mortars made a gentle rhythm. The women were going about their work, with the small children playing in the dust at their feet, while the older children banged noisily on calabashes.

This was Equiano's home and his life. You would probably find his village as tranquil today as it was then.

9

But in the forest outside the village things were not as safe as they seemed. Thieves and bandits lurked in the undergrowth. The children of the village were forbidden to venture into the forest. Most of them were scared off by the stories the grown-ups told of vicious kidnappers. But not our hero, Equiano.

One day he could no longer contain his curiosity and he slipped away to explore. 'Got him!' yelled the thieves with glee.

'Help!' cried Equiano, as he was carried away, kicking and screaming.

For almost seven months he was passed from person to person. Once a mother bought him, as a present for her son. Another time he was sold to a blacksmith for seventy cowry shells, because he wanted a boy to help him work the bellows.

Equiano adapted surprisingly well to this new life. Perhaps it was because he was intelligent and sensible. Or maybe it was because (as we know) he was very curious and always ready to try new experiences − whether it was tasting the flesh of a coconut, or trying to speak a new language.

One day some slave traders captured Equiano. They were buying (or stealing) slaves to fill the hold of their ship. Their plan was to sail to the West Indies, sell the slaves, and make a fortune.

Because Equiano had always lived in the forest, he was dazzled by his first sight of the ocean − infinite and blue − or was it green? He had a strange feeling in his stomach, which got worse when he saw the slave ship anchored out in the bay.

Until then Equiano had been too upset to notice
the strange-looking people, armed with guns and
swords, who were bustling around him. Their skin
was a pinkish colour, their hair straight and yellow,
and their language different from anything he had
ever heard before. They grabbed hold of him, and
started to examine him from all directions. They
made him open his mouth wide. They pinched his
arms and legs. Then he had to jump up and down.
What on earth was going on?

It was then that he noticed the others, chained and
crowded together in the hold of the ship. They
were staring up at him. Did they know what was
happening?

Its human cargo loaded, the ship set sail for the West Indies. The slaves were chained to the deck, where they burned up in the sun, or got soaked in the tropical storms. The voyage was unbearably long, and many of the slaves became ill. The only thing that helped to pass the time was watching the sun as it moved across the sky.

After long weeks at sea, the slave ship finally docked at Bridgetown in Barbados.

Bright posters plastered on the walls of Bridgetown announced the next sale of slaves, and boasted that the cargo was of a fine quality. There was frantic activity on the slave ship. The ship's doctor rounded up the sailors and got them to help him try to make the exhausted captives as presentable as possible before taking them ashore.

Equiano ignored them. He was fascinated by the noise and activity in the harbour, and by the tall houses that were so different from the huts at home. He was also amazed by the mysterious powers that these white people had. Look at them parading around on four-legged animals of different colours.

Suddenly there was a loud drum roll. Planters and merchants bustled into the enclosure in which the slaves had been placed. The bidding began.

The slaves that were not sold were sent to a plantation in Virginia in America. Equiano was one of these. When they arrived in Virginia, the slaves were divided up and sent to all four corners of the colony. Equiano was the only one left behind at the plantation. He felt very alone – his last connection to his roots was gone.

The sight of a young slave girl soon stopped him from feeling sorry for himself. An iron muzzle was strapped to her face – probably to stop her from stealing food from the kitchens.

Equiano found these white people very strange. They seemed to have eyes everywhere. 'Look at that,' he said to himself, 'they even put up pictures of their dead people to watch over the living.'

One day a ship's Captain called Lieutenant Henry Pascal visited the plantation. When the Lieutenant was not fighting wars, he spent his time trading with the Americas. He took a liking to Equiano, and bought him for forty pounds. They then set sail for England.

The arrival of Henry Pascal marked a turning point in Equiano's life. He could not believe the welcome that he received on his new master's ship. Equiano was not used to so much attention. Although his master was kind, he did not allow Equiano to keep his own name. Slave owners always renamed their slaves, and our hero became Gustavus Vasa. He never accepted this name so, to please him, we will continue to call him Equiano.

It was the thirteenth week of the crossing, and they were beginning to run short of food. One day Lieutenant Pascal was busy stuffing his pipe with a pleasant smelling mixture of Virginia tobacco (several bales of which were in the hold of the ship). Equiano passed him on deck, carrying a stack of plates. The Lieutenant scowled and said, 'My boy, we have a problem here, as you can see. We still have several days of sailing ahead of us and fish is scarce. Our barrels of salted foods are almost empty.'

Equiano stopped, unsure of what was coming next.

'We've come to like you very much,' Pascal continued, 'so you can imagine how sorry we'd be, if we had to ... eat you.'

Equiano was horrified. A row of sailors sitting nearby found this very funny, and burst out laughing, but our hero was not amused at all.

He would not have given this bad joke another thought, if they had not run into a raging storm that night. A sailor fell overboard and they were unable to rescue him. Equiano was terrified that the sailors might offer him as a sacrifice to the angry gods. He only relaxed when he saw the coast of England, two days later, through a thick early morning fog.

19

'Look!' shouted Equiano, 'All that salt on the quays and on the houses!'
Equiano was remembering the long trail of caravans carrying salt that
had passed his village before they set off on their routes to the north.

Lieutenant Pascal started laughing. He explained that it was snow that
covered the land like a big white carpet. Once ashore, he took Equiano
through the clusters of houses and shops, and showed him the snowed-
in alleys of the town of Falmouth.

The young boy never forgot his first year in England.
He discovered many new and exciting things and
met many interesting people. However, this
time was soon over. Equiano's master was
recalled to war. Putting on his uniform once
again, with his slave at his side, Pascal set
off to offer his services to the king.

The English fleet forged ahead at full sail. They crossed the western seas to attack the French in Quebec. The cannons thundered from the ship, destroying buildings along the seashore. Victorious, they left Quebec, and returned to the open sea.

Back in London, a young American who had become his friend welcomed Equiano. Richard Baker was four years older than Equiano, and the two young men were inseparable.

Together they took long walks through the streets of London. Richard entertained Equiano by telling him the history of the many palaces and monuments they saw. Equiano especially liked to stroll along the Thames River with the noisy overloaded ferries plying between the two banks, the barges of vegetables and fruits which supplied the markets, the commercial vessels making their way with difficulty through the continuous stream of boats of all sizes; and, best of all, the shouts of the boatmen and the spicy smells of the heavy bales arriving from the West Indies.

'Richard,' Equiano said to his friend one day, 'I have to tell you something. You know how you're always reading books? Well, I stole one of them to see what's inside. I want to know as much about the world as you do. But when I talked to your book, it didn't answer me. Is it because my skin is black?'

Richard Baker was moved by his friend's confession, and set about helping Equiano to educate himself. At the same time, Equiano decided to adopt the religion of his masters. It seemed to be the right way to become part of the society in which he was now living.

At this time there was great rivalry between France and England over who owned the colonies, and so the guns of war were never quiet for long. Equiano's master was recalled to war and, with a heavy heart, Equiano left his friend Dick to go and fight in the Mediterranean.

The number of ships involved in the fighting was unbelievable. Fighting raged from

deck to deck, ship to ship. The air was acrid with the smell of gunpowder and blood. Sailors howled as they were cut to pieces by shrapnel or thrown into the sea. Fire barges exploded, transforming the already battered ships into fiery torches. Equiano was terrified and sickened by the violence and loss of life. He quietly gave thanks that he had survived.

25

But his relief was not to last long. The ship had hardly docked before they were told to take on supplies and go the aid of the English forces that were laying siege to Belle-lle, a French Island in the English Channel. Equiano narrowly missed being injured by cannon fire, and this cured him of ever wanting to go to war again.

When he returned to civilian life, our hero was seventeen years old. He decided that he should start to think about his future. Freedom was the first thing he wanted. Then he had to find a way to earn a living, so he could continue his education and find a good job. On board ship, Equiano had found another teacher. A young officer, who had noticed Equiano's intelligence, had taught him the basics of arithmetic, and given him lessons in writing and deportment. All Equiano had to do now was convince Lieutenant Pascal to allow him to buy back his freedom.

'Lieutenant Pascal,' he began, 'I have always served you honestly, and given you my share of our spoils. You promised me . . .'

'Be quiet boy!' Lieutenant Pascal snapped, 'I didn't promise you anything. Anyway, I've just sold you. You leave on a sloop tomorrow, which will take you to the West Indies where they are expecting you.'

Tears filled Equiano's eyes. He was furious. How could his master be so unfair? All his plans had come to nothing. How long would he have to wait for freedom?

On 13 February 1763 he landed for the first time at Montserrat, a place that had a bad reputation for cruelty to slaves. He was welcomed by a jovial, pot-bellied man, dressed in an ample outfit of black serge, with a fashionable high collar and fine cambric cuffs.

Robert King, an important merchant on Montserrat, employed as many as six clerks in his warehouses, and owned a flotilla of coastal vessels. He transported sugar, rum and other merchandise that he bought from nearby islands. He was a Quaker and was known to be a man of great kindness and refinement. He disapproved of the attitude of many of the planters who were extremely brutal to their slaves. Slave owners often branded their slaves with hot irons as a sign that they belonged to them. They frequently whipped slaves until they were bleeding, or weighed them down with heavy chains to prevent them from escaping. The life of a slave was filled with humiliation – they were even sold according to how much they weighed!

Many slaves would not stand for this brutal treatment. They ran away from the plantations and took refuge in 'maroon' camps hidden deep in the forests. They lived the lives of fugitives – always terrified that they would be recaptured.

Equiano's new master treated him more like a friend than a slave, and gave him many important responsibilities. In his new role as a businessman, Equiano met two interesting men. One of these was Thomas Farmer, an Englishman who was in charge of one of the sloops trading with the islands. Equiano often travelled with him on his trips. The other was an old Creole black man, who had wandered around the Caribbean before settling down in Montserrat. He never tired of telling stories about slave society in the islands. And there was a great deal to tell.

He told Equiano of one man whose master stole his own fish from him; and of another slave who was chased and whipped by an officer he had asked for help because someone had hurt him.

The courts did not place any value on the word of a 'coloured freedman' who spoke on behalf of a slave, since the word of a black person had no value against that of a white person. Moreover, plantation owners had the right to maim, or even kill their slaves if they offended them, and the owners would not be punished.

'What can we do to stop these things?' Equiano often asked.

'Nothing, my friend. It's the law,' was the reply.

The law! How could the law be so unjust? Equiano refused to accept this unjust law. He stored up these incidents in his mind, along with the things that happened to him as a slave. Someday, surely, he would be given a chance to tell of these shameful practices.

You know, that boy is an excellent sailor – and not bad as a merchant either. He's also intelligent. Let him come and work on my ship – he'll serve you much better there than in your warehouses.

'You know, that boy is an excellent sailor – and not bad as a merchant either,' Thomas Farmer said one day to Robert King. 'He's also intelligent. Let him come and work on my ship – he'll serve you much better there than in your warehouses.'

Mr King was not happy with this idea – mainly because he thought Equiano would jump ship later. However, he was fed up with sailors who were more interested in flirting in taverns than in doing their jobs. And he knew too, that Equiano would not be lazy. So, eventually, he gave in to Thomas Farmer.

This opened up a new life for the young slave – one that was rich in adventure and filled with interesting people. Equiano travelled from island to island on his master's business, but he also did some business for himself. Little by little, he set aside the money he earned, so that one day he would be able to buy his freedom.

Equiano was driven by the thought that his freedom had
been unfairly taken from him, and he was determined
to succeed at being both a sailor and a businessman.
(It was ironic that Equiano, who so loved the sea,
could not swim, and sometimes the waves were so
dangerous that his life was at risk.) He worked
very hard – travelling to Grenada, St Eustatius,
St Kitts and Barbados. His position as a
slave and the laws in the West Indies
meant that he was often forced to
defend himself – sometimes
with his fists.

My boy, steering this boat will soon be as familiar to you as the taste of brown rum.

Thomas Farmer believed in Equiano and boasted of his abilities to anyone who would listen. Equiano accompanied him on his new sloop to Guadeloupe, and the ports of Charleston and Philadelphia on the American mainland. These trips interested Equiano more than others, because he made a lot of money that he was able to put into his savings.

Mr Farmer was also very pleased with Equiano's progress. 'My boy,' he said one day, 'steering this boat will soon be as familiar to you as the taste of brown rum.'

Their business concluded, they set off on the voyage home. Equiano spent hours daydreaming of becoming a master navigator, buying his freedom, and sailing to England. But his dreams were very different from real life as many of the passengers aboard the sloop were outraged that a black man could be given important tasks on a ship.

The ship was unloaded and the merchandise sold. Equiano could not wait another moment. He rushed into his master's office.

'Give you your freedom?' exclaimed Mr King. 'What are you thinking of? Do you have the money to buy your freedom? And where did you get it?'

The young slave confirmed that he did indeed have the forty pounds sterling and that he had earned the money honestly.

'This boy could have escaped a hundred times,' Thomas Farmer said, 'but because he's loyal, he's always remained faithful to you. He has good business sense, and he's managed to save the money he needs. He has the right to claim his due. And anyway,' he added, 'what do you have to lose?'

Mr King was speechless. He did not want to disappoint Equiano, but he also did not want to lose such a good business associate. At last he said, 'Very well, go and fetch the Freedom Papers from the Registry Office.'

Dizzy with gratitude and with tears of happiness streaming down his face, Equiano rushed out of the room.

He agreed to do two more voyages for the Captain, but this time as a 'free man'. Unfortunately, during one of these trips Captain Farmer died. Equiano was very sad, because he had loved the old man like a father. But there was little time for sorrow. The ship had no Captain and, buffeted by the wind, it was drifting off course. Gathering all his courage, and what little he had learnt about navigation, the ex-slave steered the sloop alone for ten days. He had earned himself the title of Captain.

Soon after that, on January 26, 1767, he was on the ship *Andromach* on his way to England. He was twenty years old. His future lay before him and he was free!

The voyage took seven long weeks. It was an important time for Equiano, because he had time to take stock of his life. He remembered the pink faces – sometimes kind, sometimes twisted with hatred. There were sad times he wanted to forget, but also times of true friendship. Meanwhile, the important thing was to see what kind of welcome England had in store for him.

A Free Man

It was a most unexpected welcome. Equiano had hardly set foot on the paving stones of London when he found himself face to face with none other than Lieutenant Pascal. 'Where's my share of the war booty?' Equiano demanded.

Pascal pretended not to know what he was talking about. The two men almost had a fight right there and then.

In spite of this bad start to his stay in London, Equiano wasted no time in asking around about a job. He met a hair dresser in Covent Garden, who taught him his skills – how to curl the hair of young women and powder the wigs of fashionable young men.

Equiano spent some time helping the hair dresser, but he also worked for a music teacher who taught singing and the French horn. In the evenings, he took classes in Arithmetic and Commerce. It was all like a dream.

But the life Equiano was leading had a price, and it soon became clear to our friend that he would have to find a way to earn more money. A Dr Irving, in Pall Mall, provided the solution. He was a scientist who was experimenting with ways of filtering seawater. One day, when Equiano was in his office, he noticed the young man's interest in his work.

Dr Irving generously shared his findings with him. This knowledge was to prove useful to Equiano later in his life.

In the meantime, Equiano was struggling to make ends meet. He had to stop taking his classes and find work that would pay him a decent wage.

Equiano decided to go back to sea. He joined the services of a rich gentleman who was going on a voyage and needed a hairdresser. The trip was amazing: each day brought something new. Equiano loved Italy, with its superb palaces and rich wines. The nobility of Genoa and the charm of Naples made a big impression on him. The fury of the volcano at Mount Vesuvius astonished him – he'd never seen anything like it in his life.

At Porto, he enjoyed the carnival, but was frightened by the all-powerful Portuguese Inquisition. Their journey also took them through the Greek Islands.

Smyrna, in Turkey, truly amazed Equiano: the glowing pastel minarets echoing with the calls to prayer of the muezzins, the grapes, sun-warmed and bursting with sweetness, and the alluring mystery of the women who were completely veiled. A Turkish officer even offered him two of the young women from his harem – as a sign of friendship.

But this was not a voyage for pleasure only. In each port different products were loaded on board – each of them typical of the region that they visited.

Even the most delightful experiences come to an end and, by July 1770, Equiano found himself back in England.

Equiano allowed himself a break from travel and then, in April 1777, he took a job as a steward on a sailing ship going to the West Indies. He had missed the smell of the spices and the aroma of the bales.

Unfortunately his position as 'Free coloured', of which he was very proud in England, did not protect him from the prejudice of the settlers in his business dealings in the Caribbean. In fact, he was so unsure of the situation in Jamaica that he decided to return to Europe.

Before leaving Kingston, however, Equiano attended a gathering of Africans from various tribal groups. They met at night, when they could drink and dance as a way of forgetting the sadness of their lives.

On his return to the boat, something happened which almost brought Equiano's story to an end. He was working in the hold when he absentmindedly put a candle on a barrel of gunpowder. What an explosion! Fortunately, our young hero escaped unharmed.

Equiano found himself in London again, but not for long. He was longing for the sea. He set off looking for ships' offices, going from street to street, trying to waylay the quartermasters who were in charge of hiring seamen for the voyages. He discovered that an expedition was being organised to look for a route to India by sea, via the North Pole. This was a godsend for our adventurer.

So, on 24 May 1773 Equiano set sail on the *Race Horse* – a war sloop of more than 100 tons – under the command of John Constantine Phipps.

It was a truly fantastic adventure. The ship carefully made its way through spectacular surroundings, frozen solid because of the extreme cold. Our friend was thrilled by the sight of the walruses and whales slipping into the seas around the icebergs. The commander gave Equiano the job of overseeing the crew who had to procure fresh water, and he put the skills that he had learnt from Dr Irving to good use. As a result they were able to distil up to forty gallons of water each day.

It was difficult to believe − Equiano had been a trader in Turkey and the Caribbean, a wigmaker in London, and now he was a chemist in the Arctic.

Icebergs loomed all around them. Stuck fast in the ice, they had to unload their supplies, leave them on an ice floe, and try to free the ship − all this while keeping the polar bears at bay.

Equiano survived. They did not find a route to India, but he was certainly the first African to sail through the ice-bound region of Spitzbergen.

At home, warmed by a comforting fire in the hearth, Equiano became excited again when he heard about a new project. This time he was to be part of an expedition that was going to explore the Mosquito Coast, in Honduras. And with none other than Dr Irving. They set off on 12 February 1776.

They chose a fertile piece of land next to a lagoon and began to clear an area in the forest. A tribe of Indians, who lived on the edge of their camp, was willing to barter with them. The Indians brought oil, fresh fish and turtle shells for the Englishmen. In exchange they received gallons of distilled rum made from pineapples, as well as medical care and advice on snakebites.

51

One day, an important Indian chief arrived, surrounded by his men. He claimed that he travelled from tribe to tribe, sorting out arguments or conflicts. What he was really doing was extorting sugar, rum, or gunpowder from the tribes. A great feast was held in his honour, and the rum flowed. Alligator meat was roasted on huge fires. When Equiano finally convinced himself to try it, he found it tasted very much like fresh salmon. Not too bad at all.

After a while, the daily routine became monotonous and Equiano got bored. He decided to leave Dr Irving as soon as the rainy season ended. He set off in a canoe. After paddling hard through swarms of mosquitoes, he finally reached the coast.

The winds of adventure may well continue to blow, but they will blow without me! I'm going to have a rest!

Slave traders attacked him, but Equiano escaped in a makeshift canoe. Our hero only survived because one slaver was a poor shot, and the other took pity on him.

He was picked up by a ship en route to Jamaica. The Captain was an unpleasant man, and Equiano was not well treated on board, but he did have a chance to taste unusual food again. This time it was the meat of the manatee, which tasted more like beef than fish to him.

He finally arrived back in England on 7 January 1777. His voyage to the port at Plymouth had been long and tiring, involving smoky cabins, and rude and unfriendly fellow passengers.

Equiano said to himself, 'The winds of adventure may well continue to blow, but they will blow without me! I'm going to have a rest!'

But there was to be no rest for our hero.

Equiano did not go back to sea but his life continued to be as busy as before. He gathered together his notes and, from all he had experienced, wrote the story of his life. Much of his story was aimed at fighting the evils of slavery. After the story was published, he travelled around England, working with abolitionist committees and appealing to timid parliamentarians to help put an end to slavery.

Twenty years later, he still had a twinkle in his eye, although his adventures and his disappointments had deeply marked his face.

The Militant

Equiano was talking to Major Straight, a tall, thin man with red hair. They were good friends because they were both passionate about the abolition of slavery.

'Be reasonable, my friend,' said Major Straight, 'too many meetings will exhaust you.'

Equiano, irritated, shook his head and replied, 'You know that I have to continue. There's still so much to be done — like stopping that motion that the plantation owners have put forward, and . . .'

'I know,' his friend replied. 'And there will be other battles to fight too, believe me.'

The room was getting darker as the afternoon sunlight faded. Equiano was sitting behind his desk, his back to a library filled with books and files. He was angrily writing the last pages of an article for the next day's newspaper.

The Major took a pinch from his snuffbox. Beside him sat a young man, about twenty years old, who was listening avidly to the conversation of his elders, and longing to interrupt. This young man, Clement Desnoisette, had recently arrived from France, bringing with him letters for the Major. Desnoisette was studying to be a painter.

'Don't you think, sir,' the young man said boldly, 'that the ideas of our Society of Friends of the Blacks carry a lot of weight? Men like Brissot …'

'Brissot?' interrupted Equiano. 'Let me be frank here — men like him are good thinkers, but they know nothing about what's really happening on the islands. Often they're all talk — and they don't carry much weight with the plantation owners either. Have you seen what Brissot wrote? Let me find the article.'

'Here it is! He starts by putting into perspective some of the rumours that the plantation owners are spreading about him, but then he goes on to say, and I quote, 'not only is the Society of Friends of the Blacks not seeking the abolition of slavery at this time, but it would be distressed if it were even proposed. The Blacks are not yet ready for freedom. We have to prepare them for it.' I'm willing to admit that your Brissot is against slavery, but I prefer actions to words – that's why I like the English liberals – they are prepared to do, not only to talk.'

The young Frenchman was upset. 'How can you say that the English are better at actions than words? They have fewer colonies in the islands than the French. They're just waiting to see our trade collapse and then . . .'

Major Straight burst out laughing and, trying to keep the peace, said, 'Come on, stop arguing. We have a huge task ahead of us, and if we fight each other, then we play into the enemy's hands. Our nations should work together to fight slavery.'

Clement, not wanting the Englishman to win the point, replied, 'And what do you think of the Declaration of Independence of your former colonies in America?'

Equiano smiled. 'You mean the article on the equality of men? Jefferson is a politician as well as a lawyer. Read the text again. Black slaves are excluded!'

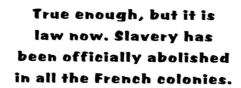

True enough, but it is law now. Slavery has been officially abolished in all the French colonies.

Equiano studied the young man for a long time. What he saw in this enthusiastic and generous young man delighted him. He could see himself as a slave at the same age, filled with the same kind of passion. 'I know that,' he said, 'but have they enforced the law over the last three years?'

'Have you read the letter I brought from General Dumas?' asked the young man.

'Of course,' Equiano replied. 'Alexander is a good friend of mine who understands my situation. He was born in the islands, and his mother was a black slave. I'm happy to hear that he is still in charge of his regiment.'

'Why does that surprise you?'

'You're too young to remember the Knight of St George. He was relieved of his command barely a few months before your famous decree was passed.'

'Why was he relieved?'

'Maybe because of the colour of his skin,' Equiano replied.

'That's unbelievable! Do you think things are any better in Sierra Leone?'

Silence was the only response that he received.

58

Major Straight cleared his throat and said quietly, 'I'd prefer to avoid that subject in the presence of our host . . . the truth is that things did not turn out well. The idea was not bad: Granville Sharp started a "Committee to Save the Black Poor". He wanted to start a colony of freed slaves in Africa. The botanist, Smeathman, was involved too.'

'I was in charge of supplies,' Equiano added.

'But our friend here soon quarrelled with Sir Irving, who was in charge of the project, and accused Sir Irving of stealing from the funds.'

'What a scoundrel!' exclaimed the young man.

The Major shook his head and said, 'The newspapers all printed the story, and Equiano was praised. But the whole thing had created a bad feeling. The Africans, who were keen to be involved in the beginning, began to suspect that something fishy was going on, and fewer and fewer showed interest. We tried very hard to overcome this, but then the organisers made the mistake of letting the ships leave too late. The rainy season and the fevers wiped out a third of the settlers after their arrival.

The rest of the settlers were depressed and angry. They decided that they'd rather be slaves than try to survive on the land they had been given.'

Equiano shook his head sadly. 'I still believe that in the future we'll find a way to trade with Africa. Someday we'll put up factories and open mines there, and teach the local people how to administer their land and their work. Africa is twice as big as Europe, and could become a huge market for our own products. I hope I live to see it. . . . what's that noise outside?'

They could hear the clanking of coach wheels and the prancing of horses, as a coach made its way up from the wharves alongside the Thames River.

The Major went over to the window. 'It looks like someone returning home – wait, it's that coloured French officer, who's just been freed. I recognise him – in fact, I arrested him years ago in St Vincent!'

'A coloured officer?' Equiano exclaimed. 'What's his name?'

It looks like someone returning home – wait, it's that coloured French officer who's just been freed.

A coloured officer? What's his name?

Captain Louis Delgrès had fought against the British in the West Indian uprising and then had been imprisoned in England for his part in this battle. The meeting between Equiano and Louis Delgrès was something to see. Both of them had overcome enormous obstacles to be where they were, both were brave and unbowed by their experiences.

And it is here that we leave our hero, Equiano, united with a brother-in-arms. Equiano – slave, merchant, wigmaker, chemist, seaman and writer. A learned man who fought injustice all his life. May he rest in peace.

A portrait beleived to be that of Olaudah Equiano (*Library of Congress*)

© 2001 Jean-Jacques Vayssières

First published in Jamaica 2001 by
Ian Randle Publishers Ltd
11 Cunningham Avenue
Kingston 6, Jamaica

A catalogue record of this book is available from
The National Library of Jamaica.

ISBN 976-637-037-0 hardcover
ISBN 976-637-029-X paperback

First published in South Africa by
New Africa Books
PO Box 23317, Claremont 7735
South Africa

New Africa Books is an imprint of New Africa Education Publishing (Pty) Ltd.

ISBN 1-919888-02-0 hardcover
ISBN 1-919888-01-2 paperback

First published in Nigeria by
Lantern Books, a division of Literamed Publications (Nig.) Ltd
Plot 45, Alausa Bus-Stop,
P.M.B. 21068, Ikeja, Lagos-State, Nigeria
Email: literamed@infoweb.abs.net

ISBN 978-142-087-1 hardcover

First published in Ghana by
Sam-Woode Ltd
P. O. Box AN 12719, Accra-North, Ghana

ISBN 9988-609-36-1 paperback

The Publishers wish to thank the following persons
for their contribution to the preparation of the manuscript:
Diane Browne, Jean Small and Marie-José N'Zengou-Tayo

Typography and cover design by ProDesign Ltd.
Red Gal Ring, Kingston, Jamaica